Strawberries

by Robin Nelson

first step nonfiction

Lerner Publications · Minneapolis

This is a strawberry.

How do strawberries grow?

Most strawberries are grown
from other strawberry plants.

First, strawberry **shoots** are planted.

The shoot grows and becomes a **seedling**.

The seedling spreads.

Then flower **buds** grow.

The strawberry plant grows
bigger.

The white flowers open.

Bees fly to the flowers.

Then a strawberry grows
where the flower was.

A **ripe** strawberry is big and red.

These strawberries are ready
to be picked.

Strawberries are good to eat.

In the winter, the plants are covered.

Next spring, new strawberries will grow on the plants.

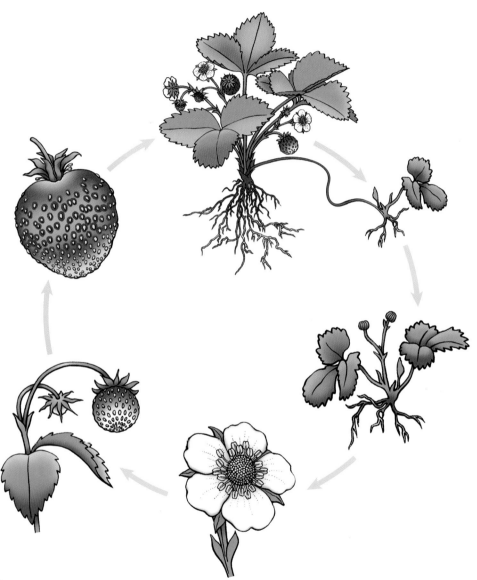

Strawberries

Some strawberry plants only have strawberries once a year. Other strawberry plants have strawberries all year. Strawberries are grown all over the world. California grows the most strawberries in the United States.

The life cycle of a strawberry is 90 days. This means shoots planted in the spring have strawberries ready to eat by early summer.

Strawberry Facts

 Strawberries are the only fruit with their seeds on the outside.

 There are about 200 seeds on the outside of each strawberry.

 If you grow strawberries from a seed, you don't plant the seed in the ground. First, you let the roots and a shoot start to grow.

Strawberries are always picked by hand so they don't get squished.

 There are many strawberry farms around the world where you can pick your own strawberries.

 May is National Strawberry Month.

Glossary

 buds – a flower that has not opened yet

 ripe – ready to eat

 seedlings – young plants

 shoots – plants that have just started to grow

Index

The images in this book are used with the permission of:© Tombaky/Dreamstime.com, p. 2; © Achilles/Dreamstime.com, p. 3; © Karlene Schwartz, pp. 4, 22 (second from bottom); © Todd Strand/Independent Picture Service, pp. 5, 22 (bottom); © Dwight Kuhn , pp. 6, 7, 9; © Down the Garden Path/Alamy, p. 8; © Pasquale Mingarelli/Alamy, p. 10; © iStockphoto.com/ Chepko, p. 11; © Kim Karpeles/Alamy, p. 12; © Grant Heilman Photography/Alamy, p. 13; © Inga Spence/Photo Researchers, Inc., p. 14; © John Birdsall/The Image Works, p. 15; © FourT4/Alamy, p. 16; © Francis Jalain/Jupiterimages, p. 17; Illustrations by © Laura Westlund/Independent Picture Service.
Front cover:© iStockphoto.com/Ron Hohenhaus.

Lerner Publications Company
A division of Lerner Publishing Group, Inc.
241 First Avenue North
Minneapolis, MN 55401 USA

For reading levels and more information, look up this title at www.lernerbooks.com.

Library of Congress Cataloging-in-Publication Data

Nelson, Robin, 1971–
    Strawberries / by Robin Nelson.
      p.   cm. — (First step nonfiction. Plant life cycles)
    Includes index.
    ISBN: 978–0–7613–4074–4 (lib. bdg. : alk. paper)
    ISBN: 978–0–7613–5176–4 (EB pdf)
    1. Strawberries—Life cycles—Juvenile literature. I. Title. II. Series.
  SB385.N45 2009
  634'.75—dc22   2008033739

Manufactured in the United States of America
6-41737-10133-7/1/2016